# Table of Contents

# MEET YOUR YARD MONSTERS

There is a jungle right outside your door. You can't see most of them, but your yard is crammed with trillions of tiny creatures. They're everywhere—in the air, on the ground, and all over the compost heap. They're in the plants and even inside the bugs crawling on the plants!

bacteria microbes in soil

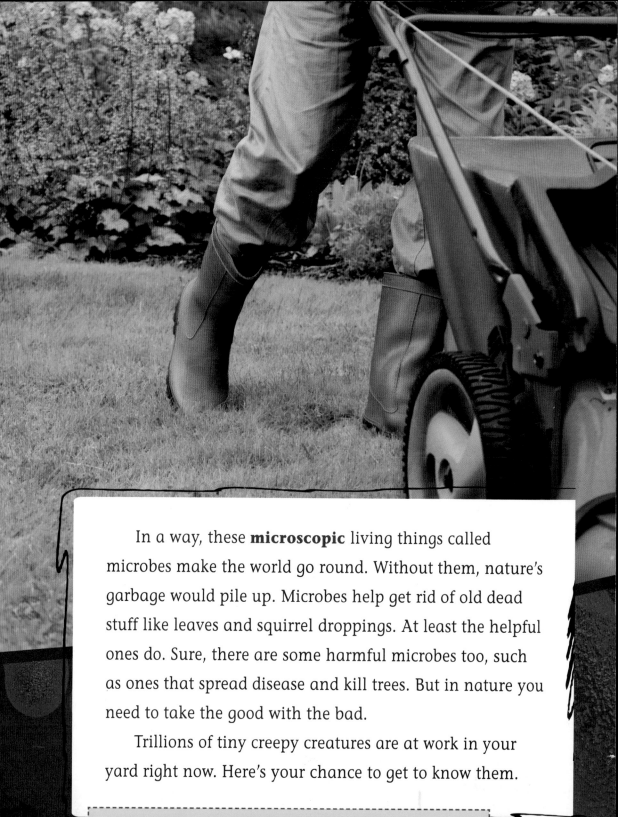

In a way, these **microscopic** living things called microbes make the world go round. Without them, nature's garbage would pile up. Microbes help get rid of old dead stuff like leaves and squirrel droppings. At least the helpful ones do. Sure, there are some harmful microbes too, such as ones that spread disease and kill trees. But in nature you need to take the good with the bad.

Trillions of tiny creepy creatures are at work in your yard right now. Here's your chance to get to know them.

**microscopic**—too small to be seen without a microscope

# Chapter 1
# GARDEN GOBBLERS

Whether you have a garden full of prize-winning roses or just a patch of grass, microbes are making things happen in your yard. In 1 gram of soil alone, there are as many as 1 billion busy bacteria cells.

We've all heard of bacteria that can give you strep throat or food poisoning. But there are many kinds of bacteria in the world, and they're not all bad. Not by a long shot! These one-celled creatures help give plants the materials they need to grow. Some bacteria help soil hold more water, which is also important to plants.

Other types of bacteria are **decomposers**. These bacteria clean up dead plants and other natural matter, like that dog poop you almost stepped in. Decomposers take in the **nutrients** from nature's garbage. Then they put the nutrients back into the soil through their waste. This process frees up the nutrients for other plants to use.

soil bacteria

**decomposer**—an organism that lives off dead or decaying material
**nutrient**—a substance needed by a living thing to stay healthy

gray mold on strawberry

# FUZZY FUNGUS

What's gray, fuzzy, and not tasty dipped in chocolate? The strawberries in your garden if they get gray mold. Yuck! Gray mold, also called Botrytis fruit rot, is caused by a **fungus**. It can make your strawberries and other fruits get rotten and squishy.

Mold spores are microscopic. You can only see them when they start to grow and multiply. Once mold finds a good food source, it reproduces and spreads. It creates an entire fuzzy family of spores. Rotting happens after the mold starts breaking down the plant.

## MICRO-FACT!

A fungus called late blight attacked Ireland's potato crop in the 1800s. It destroyed nearly half of the country's potatoes. More than 1 million people left the country. Up to 1 million others starved.

# WORM WARRIORS

Your soil is crawling with little critters called nematodes. These tiny worms are no bigger than the head of a pin. Root-knot nematodes sneak inside plant roots and remove nutrients, destroying healthy crops.

Other nematodes are friendlier. They actually save gardens from harmful insects. They wiggle inside pests like maggots, cutworms, rootworms, and white grubs. The nematodes inject bacteria that kill the pests. Then they eat the insects' insides.

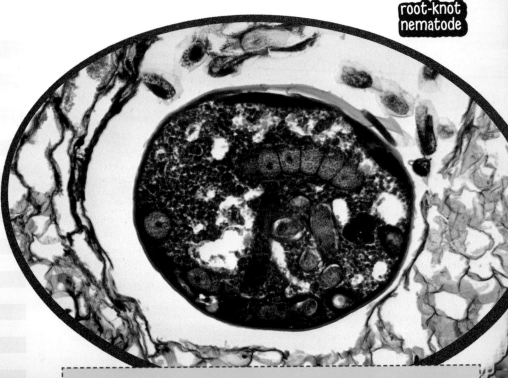

root-knot nematode

**fungus**—a living thing that is a decomposer and needs moisture; molds, mildews, yeasts, and mushrooms are fungi

# Chapter 2

# TREE TOPPLERS

Everybody likes trees, right? They're pretty and they make shade. They're also delicious if you're a bark beetle. The beetles aren't harmful, but the microbes they bring with them are.

In the mid-1900s, Dutch elm disease came to the United States, killing more than 70 million elm trees. A fungus carried by bark beetles was to blame. The beetles passed it from tree to tree as they fed, slowly killing the trees. Many towns looked bare and empty after their huge elm trees were wiped out. Plant experts are still working to find a cure for this tree disease.

## MICRO-FACT!

Some trees have their own helpful microbes. In areas with poor soil, some trees grow special bacteria at their roots. These bacteria help enrich the soil, providing nutrients the trees need to grow.

elm bark beetle

dead elm trees

# FIRE BLIGHT

Apple and pear trees make excellent climbing trees. They're also excellent homes for bacteria that cause a disease called fire blight. The bacteria infect the trees and turn their leaves and blossoms brown or black. The leaves look like they burned in a fire, which is how this plant disease got its name.

Severe cases of fire blight can destroy the entire tree. Wind, rain, or insects may carry fire blight from sick trees to healthy ones. These bacteria especially love warm, wet weather.

**MICRO-FACT!**
Fire blight can cause a tree's fruit to ooze reddish slime.

apple tree with fire blight

# SPIDER MITES

You've met some fungi and bacteria. Now let's meet some mites. Spider mites are bigger than microbes, but they are still very tiny. They are only about one-half of a millimeter long—about as big as a speck of pepper. That's good because if they were bigger, these eight-legged, spidery creatures could cause big nightmares.

Spider mites may be small, but they're not harmless. In very large groups, they can destroy trees. These mites can also gobble up your grass and garden, leaving them dead or damaged.

# Chapter 3

# WEE WATER BEASTS

You're surrounded by blobs! With jelly-like movements, they change shape. When they're ready to eat, they surround bacteria or other food and suck it in. These blobs aren't science fiction monsters. They're amoebas—tiny, one-celled life-forms that live in water and wet soil. There may be up to 1 million of them in a single spoonful of dirt.

Sometimes these miniature monsters can be dangerous to you. *Acanthamoeba*, a widespread amoeba, can be found in pools, ponds, hot tubs, and even tap water. It can cause rare but severe infections in the eyes, brain, or spinal cord.

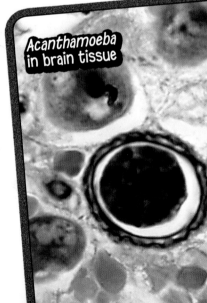

Acanthamoeba in brain tissue

## MICRO-FACT!

People with diarrhea shouldn't use pools. They may have a parasite, which can spread. If you swallow any of the parasites in the water, you'll get sick too.

**parasite**—a small organism that lives on or inside a person or animal and causes harm

# HURRAY FOR ALGAE!

You often see **algae** in lakes and oceans. But if you have a pond or even a puddle in your backyard, you might also have algae. Believe it or not, these slimy creatures help us breathe. That's because of microscopic diatoms. Diatoms are a part of the algae family. These one-celled microbes get their energy from the sun. Similar to plants, diatoms take in **carbon dioxide** we don't need and release oxygen we do need. Together, diatoms produce about 20 percent of the world's oxygen.

algae

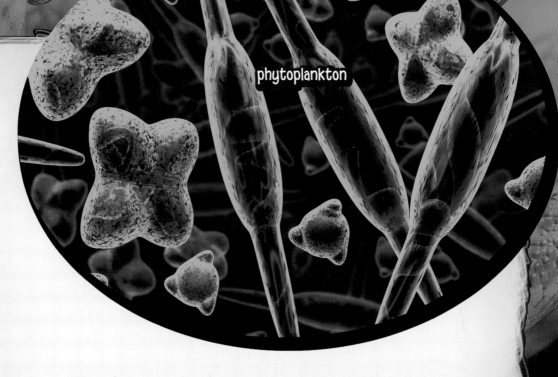

phytoplankton

Tiny diatoms also form a base in the food chain. Massed together with countless other microbes, diatoms become **phytoplankton**. In larger bodies of water, snails, fish, and tadpoles eat phytoplankton. In puddles and birdbaths, insects feed on phytoplankton. These insects then serve as food for frogs, bats, and other animals in your yard.

## MICRO-FACT!

You've probably eaten algae. It's in dozens of foods, such as pudding, cheese, chocolate milk, and ice cream.

**algae**—small organisms that live in wet places and get their energy from the sun
**carbon dioxide**—a gas in the air that animals give off and plants use to make food
**phytoplankton**—different kinds of one-celled organisms that live in water and provide food for larger creatures

# MOST DANGEROUS BEAST

There might be more than algae in that puddle. It could also be home to one of the deadliest animals in the world. It weighs less than your fingernail and it's only a few millimeters long. But it can kill you. It's killed before, and it will again.

It is the female mosquito. She can carry germs such as **viruses** or parasites. The mosquito picks up these germs after biting a sick person. When she bites again, she can inject the germs into her new victim.

**MICRO-FACT!**
Only the female mosquito bites people. She needs a blood meal before laying eggs.

**virus**—a germ that copies itself inside the body's cells

In 1905, mosquitoes spread the deadly yellow fever virus in New Orleans, killing hundreds of people in just a few months. In New York in 1999, mosquitoes began spreading an illness called West Nile virus. Since then, mosquitoes have spread the virus to hundreds of Americans each year. Mosquitoes also can carry a rare but serious virus called eastern equine encephalitis. This virus can spread to horses and humans.

In Africa and in other hot and humid parts of the world, mosquitoes spread malaria. This very dangerous disease is caused by the *Plasmodium* parasite. Malaria is the most widespread disease spread by mosquitoes today. There are about 250 million cases of malaria every year and more than 1 million deaths from the disease.

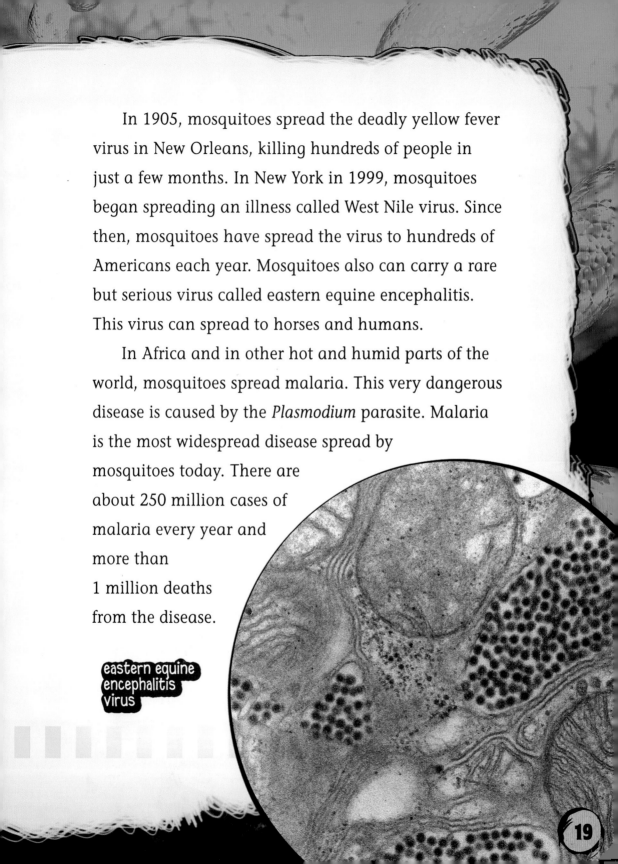

eastern equine encephalitis virus

# Chapter 4
# POOP, PETS, AND PESTS

Bird songs are delightful. Bird poop is not. Some bird droppings carry the microscopic fungus *Histoplasma capsulatum*. It grows in soil where many bird droppings fall and thrives in damp, shady spots.

Unfortunately, this fungus could be bad news for you or your cat or dog. It can infect the lungs, causing chest pain, coughing, and breathing problems. To protect yourself, wear a mask when you rake up old wet leaf piles.

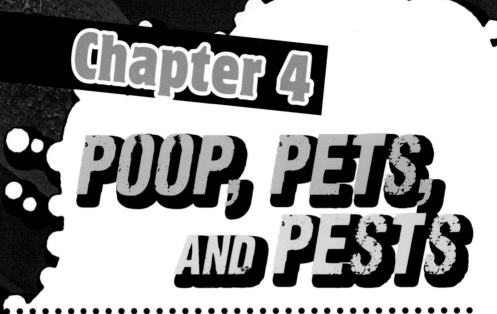

bird dropping

*Histoplasma capsulatum*

# FLEAS AND TICKS

No creepy creature tour would be complete without fleas and ticks. These tiny parasites can be found in grassy or wooded areas. Fleas hop onto furry animals, and ticks will latch onto fur or human skin. Then fleas and ticks get busy sucking the animal's blood. That's bad enough. What's worse is that these little pests can carry germs that may cause serious diseases.

tick feeding on a dog

Fleas can infect your pet with microscopic flatworms called tapeworms. Inside your pet, these parasites can grow to more than 3 feet (0.9 meter) long. Tapeworm infection may show up as tiny white worms in your pet's poop.

Fleas can also spread bacteria that cause cat scratch disease. The bacteria don't usually affect cats. But if your cat passes these bacteria along to you, they can make you very sick.

flea

## MICRO-FACT!
Fleas are expert jumpers. They can jump more than 150 times their own length.

Ticks are small, eight-legged creatures that can spread the bacteria that cause Lyme disease. Symptoms include rash, joint pain, and other problems. Another bacterium ticks may carry can cause a serious disease called Rocky Mountain spotted fever.

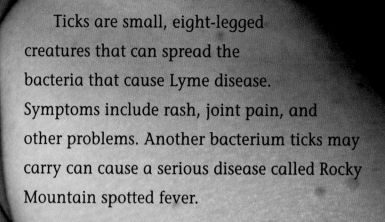

Lyme disease rash

western black-legged tick

# Chapter 5

# MICROBES COMPOST THE MOST

Ever thought about what's going on in a compost pile? It's like magic. Garbage goes in, and rich soil called humus comes out. Who performs that great magic trick? Microbes do. Billions of them.

These busy microbes break down, or decompose, a mix of food, garbage, grass clippings, and other natural material. First mesophilic bacteria start the job. Then thermophilic bacteria take over.

Both of these bacteria eat, make more bacteria, and die so fast that they produce heat. The faster the microbes work, the more heat they produce. All this heat helps to break down the hard parts of plants into mushy humus.

compost
pile

two types
of compost
bacteria

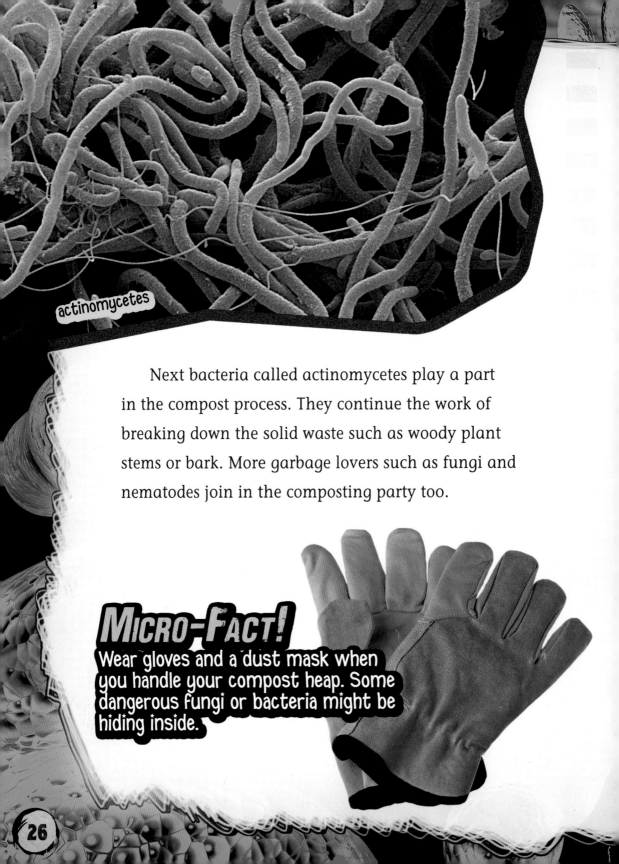

actinomycetes

Next bacteria called actinomycetes play a part in the compost process. They continue the work of breaking down the solid waste such as woody plant stems or bark. More garbage lovers such as fungi and nematodes join in the composting party too.

## MICRO-FACT!

Wear gloves and a dust mask when you handle your compost heap. Some dangerous fungi or bacteria might be hiding inside.

# STIRRING WORMS

Don't forget the earthworms. They squirm all through your compost, working like little spoons to stir and mix the mess. They gobble the garbage and then they poop. In fact, they poop as much as their own body weight every 24 hours. Luckily worm poop, called castings, is great for soil.

But don't give worms all the credit. Bacteria that live inside the worms are helping here too. When a worm eats and the garbage passes through its body, the bacteria help turn the garbage into super-rich humus.

earthworms

worm
castings

From the steaming compost pile to the tops of the trees to deep in the dirt, zillions of microbes are living it up. These microbes have been on Earth for billions of years, and they're here to stay. They'll continue to help us out by recycling our garbage and growing our plants. And we'll continue to fight them when they cause harm.

Good or bad, microbes do pretty amazing things for being so small. Next time you step in a puddle, mow the lawn, or dig in the dirt, remember the microscopic jungle bustling around you.

nematode

# Glossary

**algae** (AL-jee)—small organisms that live in wet places and get their energy from the sun

**carbon dioxide** (KAHR-buhn dye-AHK-side)—a gas in the air that animals give off and plants use to make food

**decomposer** (dee-kuhm-PO-zur)—an organism that lives off dead or decaying matter

**fungus** (FUHN-guhs)—a living thing that is a decomposer and needs moisture; molds, mildews, yeasts, and mushrooms are fungi

**microscopic** (mye-kro-SKAH-pik)—too small to be seen without a microscope

**nutrient** (NEW-tree-uhnt)—a substance needed by a living thing to stay healthy

**organism** (OR-guh-niz-uhm)—a living thing such as a plant, animal, bacterium, or fungus

**parasite** (PAIR-uh-site)—a small organism that lives on or inside a person or animal and causes harm

**phytoplankton** (FITE-oh-plangk-tuhn)—different kinds of one-celled organisms that live in water and provide food for larger creatures

**virus** (VYE-russ)—a germ that copies itself inside the body's cells

# Read More

**Crewe, Sabrina.** *In the Backyard.* Under the Microscope. New York: Chelsea House, 2010.

**Parker, Steve.** *Cocci, Spirilla & Other Bacteria.* Kingdom Classifications. Minneapolis: Compass Point Books, 2009.

**Silverman, Buffy.** *Composting: Decomposition.* Do It Yourself. Chicago: Heinemann Library, 2008.

# Internet Sites

FactHound offers a safe, fun way to find Internet sites related to this book. All of the sites on FactHound have been researched by our staff.

Here's all you do:

Visit *www.facthound.com*

Type in this code: 9781429665339

# Index